Voices on the Wind

Heather Smith

BookLeaf Publishing

India | USA | UK

Presentation by *BookLeaf Publishing*

Web: www.bookleafpub.com

E-mail: info@bookleafpub.com

ISBN: 9789358314854

First edition 2023

North Wind

I lost my voice
To the North Wind,
And it was a long time
In returning.

My heart ceased its beating
In grief at my loss.
Time moved slowly,
Sluggishly,
As if its inspiration was gone.
It was an eternity
I was lost,
Alone,
Without a soul.

Praise be the day
It returned to me
Bringing new life,
A reason to be.
May I never leave its
Warm embrace again.

Keepsake

There are so many moments
I wish I could pack up
Like charms in a jewelry box.
I could take them out
And put them on display
Whenever I wish to,
Or keep them locked up
Away from prying eyes,
Ever safe from harm.

But instead, the moments pass
Caught on a whispering breeze,
Drifting away into oblivion.
There is nothing to catch hold of,
No treasure trove,
Only a shifting sea of memories:
A fading shadow of what was.

Gone

I wonder
Why I'm here now
Alone
As always.

Despair is my companion;
It holds me close
And my heart aches
With the force of its embrace.
It threatens to crush me,
And though I fight
I know it's stronger than me.

Where are you?
Each day
I feel smaller,
More insignificant
Maybe tomorrow
I'll be
Gone
Too.

A Reminder

For so long you were the center of
My Life,
My World,
My Everything.
In that time you had the courage
To help me grow,
To let me make mistakes,
And to guide me whenever you could.

Eventually I grew up, became independent,
And we all moved forward.
It was inevitable that we would drift apart,
But even now I need you:
Your advice,
Your acceptance,
Your love.

As I look back at the journey that brought me
here,
I know that I couldn't have made it without you.
It may not seem like much,
But I give you these words
For they are timeless,
Eternal.
May they always be there to remind you,
I Love You.

Unlovely

Resentment,
Anger,
Or is it Hate
That I see in your eye?
Only you know,
And you will not tell-
The sting
Of your hand striking my face
Stays with me.
Even though I am older now,
And far away from you,
Part of me is still there
With you,
Small,
Insignificant,
And unlovely.
All I ever wanted
Was to please you,
For then you would have to love me-
Wouldn't you?
I could not succeed,
I know that now,
But still I feel like a failure:
For how can anyone else love me
If I couldn't be loved by You?

Alone

You say you listen,
But you do not hear.

My hand reaches for you,
But you cannot see.

Loneliness surrounds me,
But you turn away.

"Don't leave!" I whisper.
But I am alone.

I cry out into the darkness,
But you are not there.

Illusions of Reality

The pictures fade
But the images remain
Embedded forever in the mind's eye;
They are changing thoughts,
Warping views,
Leaving uncertainty
Of what is real.
As the focus shifts
And colour fades to grey
Right and wrong merge,
Until there is no difference.

The Pebble

Your eyes are open
But you cannot see
What is right in front of you.

I am but a pebble
In your shoe;
Insignificant,
Not even worth the effort
It takes to shake me out
Onto the ground in front of you,
For if you did
Then you might shift your focus,
For even an instant,
And then you might see
Me.

Beyond the Abyss

The world is a canyon's edge
Blurred by a misty haze.
Any step can throw you
Down into the abyss.
How do you choose the right path,
The path that leads you safely home,
When the world is a contradiction
Misleading, seducing, luring you away
Into the illusions,
The warped fantasies of others?
Where is the guardian angel,
The voice of reason,
The guide that can lead us?
Night is descending;
Will no one save us
From the approaching darkness?

At the Precipice

Falling, Falling
Slowly down
Fluttering smoothly
Toward the ground.

Softly drifting
In the breeze
Settling down
Under the trees.

Toxic smoke
Far and wide
Stealing breath,
Nowhere to hide.

Cold stone
In a maze,
Horizon shifting
In the haze.

Gloom and darkness
All around,
Stealing hope
And muffling sound.

In the distance
An angry glow
Is slithering closer,
We watch it grow.

Searing, scorching,
Raging flames
Devouring everything
They can claim.

Ashes, ashes
Falling down,
Fluttering swiftly
To the ground.

Differences

How can you hate me
For being myself
When you don't even know
Who I am?
I've never met you,
But all you can see is that
I look different,
Live different,
Act different than You.
Come closer.
Talk to me.
Look at my life
For what it is:
Uniquely beautiful.
I contribute to this society,
Because I am different
Than You,
And Him,
And them.
You aren't the same
As everyone else,
Why must I be like You?

Darkness

The air is cold in the darkness.
Each step is a journey
Away from you,
Away from me.
I am searching
For something unknown.
I have questions
But whom shall I ask?
There are so many people
Trying to influence me,
Help me,
Confuse me.
Whom should I believe?
You?
Them?

Maybe the darkness is my only friend:
It is constant,
Unswerving,
Engulfing me
In its peaceful stillness.
It comforts me,
Holds me,
Shields me.
It's my only sanctuary.

Why

It is a whispered word,
A sigh, a sob.
It's not fair, not right.
How could this happen?

Memories are faded voices
Taunting me, wounding me,
Leaving a jagged scar
That can never heal.

Pictures,
Snapshots of how life was
Before you left;
It will never be the same.

If only I could go back,
Step into that world,
Only for a moment,
To say what was left unsaid.

I hated you.
You used me, you hurt me.
I offered my help
And you walked all over me.

I loved you,
But when I reached out my hand
I was always afraid
You would let me down.

Now you have gone,
And I don't know what to do.
Thoughts race through my mind
Making me question what is real.

Part of me wonders:
If I had loved you more,
Helped you more,
Could I have saved you?

Or would you have
Dragged me down with you,
Into the abyss,
Never to re-emerge?

Crazy Contradiction

I'm angry with you
For doing
What you do.
You drive me crazy;
I want you to change,
Be like me,
Think like me,
Act like me.

Why do I feel this way?
What attracted me to you
Was how different we were
From each other.
It's not logical.
I'm a walking contradiction,
But I can't help it.
I want you to change,
Stay the same.

Glimmer in the Dark

Life is a horror movie,
Terrifying and unpredictable.
No one is safe:
Evil waits around the corner,
Watching,
Waiting,
A predator ready to strike.
It takes hope,
Destroys peace,
And leaves fear and paranoia in its place.

The sun's blinding glare is the enemy,
A burning reminder of the wounds
That don't go away;
It's a spotlight shining down
On the world,
On You,
On Me.
But he is invisible,
Unlike the scars that mar
My body,
My mind,
My soul.

I only feel safe here

In my protective cage,
This personal prison,
This enforced sanctuary.
The moon's cool gaze
Can't reach me here.
Its unblinking stare can't penetrate
These walls.
No judgements can be made,
No blame placed. Why didn't I fight harder?
How could I have let this happen?
It is my fault.
My fault...

The courage may come,
As time passes,
To take the steps to freedom.
It's a hard journey,
But I will find my way
One day.
The prize will be the simple wonders,
The gentle goodness,
The unique beauty
Of this world.
I can't see it now,
But it shines there,
In the distance:
A glimmer in the darkness.

Together

Do you remember
How effortless things used to be
When first we were together?
Just being with you
Made me feel alive and happy.
I knew that as long as we were together
Everything would work out.

I'm not sure when it happened
But somehow our relationship,
Which once felt invulnerable,
Cracked leaving a small gap
Just big enough to allow
Misunderstandings to push us apart.

Now we struggle to:
Keep the peace,
Regain the joy,
Find the familiarity,
Which was once so easy.

How can we mend the flaw
That allowed this to happen.
Can we find our way back?
Or should we move forward,
And see where the future leads?

Time heals all wounds,
Even wounds of the heart.
Take my hand,
Walk with me.
Let's see where this journey
Will take us

Emptiness

Entrenched in the darkness of night
I dream that you hold me
In your loving embrace.
My heart shies,
Spooked by the ghost
Of a memory I don't want to see.

Rain is slowly splattering
On the sill of the window
As I wake and turn to you,
Hoping to take comfort
From the warmth of your touch.
There is only emptiness
Where you once lay.

The Burden

I wish I could disappear,
Fade away into the background,
Like a chameleon.
There would be no expectations,
I couldn't let you down,
So I wouldn't see that look in your eyes.

I can't be that person,
The one you dreamed for me.
I've tried, but I don't know how.
Why can't you just accept me as I am?
A secretary, a wife, a mother.
A daughter, a sister, a friend.

Each of these are so easy, so hard.
I work each day to be the best I can,
But I'm not sure I can ever truly succeed.
I know there are "better" jobs
But this is my life,
The life I have chosen.

I just want you to be happy for me
And let me live my life my way.
If you want what's best for me,
Remove that burden off my shoulders,

And trust in my ability to know me,
Just as you know yourself.

The Guardian

A quiet guardian
Sitting quietly, holding vigil,
To be there for her charge.
She holds his hand
And the pain and nightmares stay away.
She is unseen by her sleeping ward,
But still her presence brings peace and love.
She whispers, "If love is all that holds you here,
You will have mine to the end of time."

Walk With Me

Take my hand and walk with me.
Walk with me as you did at three,
Swinging hands and singing with glee,
Every step an adventure of a journey.
Where will we go, what will we see?
Only time can foresee,
Will we climb that tree?
Maybe we can learn to ski.
The only thing that matters is: we are free
For you to be you, and for me to be me.

The Cycle

Thoughtful gifts and shared laugher,
Gave way to sneering looks and toxic words
Dripping their stinging, burning venom.
Stupid, Incompetent,
Don't you ever think?
Why can't you do anything right?
A monkey can do this better than you!
Where else would you go?
Who would want you?
You are worthless, nothing.

Soft Caresses and warm embraces
Turned to rough handling,
And quick, striking anger.
No, please stop.
I didn't mean to-
I can do better.
Let me go,
You're hurting me.

Soft comfort and warm love,
Shifted to harsh reality
And icy despair.
A hard, cold floor beneath your cheek,
Bleeding, bruised, and broken.

I need to go, to get away.
But where would I go?
Who could want me?
I am worthless, alone.
I brought this upon myself.
It is what I deserve.
Don't I?